Poetry After Lunch

Poems to Read Aloud

Poetry After Lunch

Poems to Read Aloud

Compiled by
Joyce Armstrong Carroll & Edward E. Wilson

That is question now;
And then comes answer like an Absey book.

King John, i, 1
Shakespeare

ABSEY & CO.
SPRING, TX

In Memoriam
"The Curfew tolls the knell of parting day..."
for Floyd Irving, a dear friend of teachers,
students, books, and most especially NJWPT.
It is fitting he be remembered here
among the pages of a book
and deep within the soul of poetry.

for Eddie
"I am content to live it all again
And yet again. . .
We must laugh and we must sing,
We are blest by everything. . ."
--Wm. B. Yeats
J.A.C.

for Joyce
because you took "the apple in exchange,"
and for all that time it's been nothing
but gravy, for without you,
"all the toys of the world would break."
E. E. W.

Queries regarding rights and permissions should be addressed to:

Absey & Co., Inc.
23011 Northcrest
Spring, Texas 77389
281-257-2340

Published by Absey & Co., Spring, Texas.
Manufactured in the United States of America

ISBN 1-888842-03-2 (paper)

Contents

v

Light Snacks

Pastas

Sandwiches

Salads

Daily Specials

Entrées

Children's Menu

Introduction

Compiling a poetry book ranks first among intimidating feats. First, because poetry, in and of itself, lives as an elusive, indefinable art, very often with a single word conveying the whole substance of the poem. First, too, because the grammatical-syntactical structures of poetry stir some of the most evocative images ever devised by authors. Yet, here we sit attempting to introduce that which defies introduction. For, in truth, poetry, if we believe Robert Frost, "is a fresh look and a fresh listen."

Yet, our introduction builds upon that very notion of a "fresh listen." Frost's phrase encapsulates what we love most when working with poetry and students—of all ages—those fresh looks, fresh reads, fresh listens. What began as a way of giving our audience a chance to settle in after lunch, became a ritual, a tradition of fresh listens. A tradition never to be ignored, "Aren't you going to read some poetry today?"

As you make your way through this collection, we invite you to read aloud to your audience, watch their faces when you say Andrew Hudgins' lines:

They got three years suspended sentence each
and Daddy got another tale of how
Christians are saints and strangers in the world.

Or notice the grins start and spread like marmalade when folks hear Marge Piercy's:

... I want to dance
graceful in my tonnage like Poussin nymphs.
Those melon bellies...

Taste what happens in the mouth when you read Maxine Kumin's:

She, the rosy girl in a Renoir painting.
I, an old Jew.

Whisper the final words of the Updike poem:

Good dog.

Hear the giggle within a giggle when you read the lines by Naomi Shihab Nye:

Once I knew a man who gave his wife
two skunks for a valentine.

Have fun, as your listeners will, when you emphasize the word *dive* in Peter Klappert's poem "Craft Lost in Texas." Move with the rhythm of Olga Samples Davis' "Sister Girl" or bow to the reverence of Vassar Miller's poem "On Opening One Eye."

Each poem compiled here invites collaboration. Simply put, within each poem lives the poet and the listener. We mean to encourage that collaboration through poetry's oral and most ancient roots. We mean to awaken in listeners the pleasure of the poem, pleasure not unlike that of children when they handclap beats; when they mouth sounds: *nap, tap, rap;*

when they echo words; when they squeal with wonder, awe, suspense; or when they snuggle in for the lullaby. As John Ciardi puts it, children "come prepared for delight." Just watch toddlers bob their bodies to "rub-a-dud-dub," or observe kindergartners as they chant "rain, rain, go away," or try not to smile when second graders (quite literally) belly laugh at a Prelutsky poem. When you do, you will come close to understanding the way poetry must have been received before it was ever written—actively, through the ear.

During a visit to a graduate class at Rutgers University in the early 70's, John Ciardi chose to speak about how kids receive his children's poems, specifically the "Stranger in the Pumpkin" from his book *The Man Who Sang the Sillies*. By way of example, Ciardi told about a time when he read it to a second grade class. "The kids laughed spontaneously in the spirit of its nonsense verse, so I asked them, 'Who is the stranger in the pumpkin?' In unison, they roared, 'A jack-o-lantern!'"

His message to us, however, was in the rest of the story.

As he left the building, a friend spotted him and begged a cameo appearance at the adjacent secondary campus. "Just say a few words or read a poem to my advanced twelfth graders," he cajoled. Sparked by the glow of the little ones, Ciardi thought it would be fun to try the same poem with these "big" kids. And so he did. "Who is the stranger in the pumpkin?" he asked again. Stares. Quiet. Some nervous looks and uncomfortable squirms. Finally, Ciardi said, "One stalwart young oaf in the back of the room blurted, 'Is it symbolism?'"

His point: If you want to enjoy a poem, enjoy it. Savor it. There will be time for analyzing it; there will be time for the poem to reveal its layers because the poem *is* sense. (Archibald MacLeish reminds us "A poem must not mean, but be.") And so, like the adage, "We learn to read by reading; we learn to write by writing," we learn to read poetry by reading poetry; we learn to delight in poetry by listening to it.

Through this collection, we hope listeners experience delight, but by delight, we do not mean frivolity. We have discovered that serious, very serious poems also convey delight—a different delight, the delight of identification, satisfaction, realization, comfort, or quite simply the Greek idea of catharsis—a purging of sorrow through the aesthetic of the word.

So this is no volume of poesy. Rather it embraces life, batters it, captures it, propels it in unique and complicated ways through words on a page.

Both contemporary and varied, *Poetry After Lunch: Poems to Read Aloud* offers a menu of color, texture, spice, sweetness, piquancy, richness, and tang. An abundance of tastes and flavors should suit the palate of discriminating readers. From the crusty to the simple, from the luscious to the quick and easy, this collection renders something for every need. When you are in a pinch, when you want to try something new, or when you are looking for favorite fare, just turn to the index and make your choice. Then, when you read your selection aloud, the collaboration will begin, and the poems will make love to the ear.

JAC

EEW

Troubleshooting

> Now wait—

If you close this book, one page
will touch the page across, a word
will touch another word.

Just think that kiss across
the page, how clenched it is—
and all we say is, and deep,

What you say, and I say, X-ray remarks
jumbled at once. We don't mean things
just one by one, but give and take,

Your eyes, my lips, your ears, my
heart. This book takes them,
to press, to keep.

Now start.

William Stafford

The Bookstall

Just looking at them
I grow greedy, as if they were
freshly baked loaves
waiting on their shelves
to be broken open—that one
and that—and I make my choice
in a mood of exalted luck,
browsing among them
like a cow in sweetest pasture.

For life is continuous
as long as they wait
to be read—these inked paths
opening into the future, page
after page, every book
its own receding horizon.
And I hold them, one in each hand,
a curious ballast weighting me
here to the earth.

Linda Pastan

Mother's Biscuits

In a big bowl she'd fluff in flour,
Make a fist-dent
For buttermilk and lard which she squeezed
Between her fingers
The way a child goes at a mud puddle,
Raking dry flour
From the sides until it mixed right.

She'd give the dough a pat for luck,
Nip a springy bud,
Roll it round and flat-it-down
With a motion
Continued to a grease-shined pan.
Mother's biscuits
Cooked high, crusty, with succulent middles
That took attention
At company dinners; but on kitchen-nights
They were finest
Soaked with pot liquor or gravy.

And those rich biscuits could put a shine
On Sunday patent
That let the Lord know who was there.
A panful stood
Ready as magic at dawn's light:
I'd take some
When leaving late to the schoolbus
And up the road
I'd run, puffing through biscuit crumbs
My haloed breath
Into the skin-sharp morning air.

Freda Quenneville

Young Nun at Bread Loaf

Sister Elizabeth Michael
has come to the Writers' Conference.
She has white habits like a summer sailor
and a black notebook she climbs into nightly
to sway in the hammock of a hundred knotted poems.
She is the youngest nun I have ever known.

When we go for a walk in the woods
she puts on a dimity apron that teases her boottops.
It is sprigged with blue flowers.
I wear my jeans and sneakers. We are looking
for mushrooms (chanterelles are in season)
to fry and eat with my drinks, her tomato juice.

Wet to the shins with crossing
and recrossing the same glacial brook, a mile
downstream we find them, the little pistols,
denser than bandits among the tree roots.
Forager, she carries the basket.
Her hands are crowded with those tough yellow thumbs.

Hiking back in an unction of our own sweat
she brings up Christ. Christ, that canard!
I grind out a butt and think of the waiting bourbon.
The sun goes down in disappointment.
You can say what you want, she says.
You live as if you believe.

Sister
Sister Elizabeth Michael
says we are doing Christ's work, we two.
She, the rosy girl in a Renoir painting.
I, an old Jew.

Maxine Kumin

Appetizers

Sister Girl

Sister Girl
Got it honestly...

    Mustard seed faith
    Wildcat spirit
    Wholesale humor
    Gift for gab.

    Had a laugh
    That brought you full circle
    Body soft and giving
    Like a newborn.

    She was
    Fighter quick
    Mother wit strong
    Woman/Child/Lady
    With a *No Trespassing* sign
    In full view.

Sister Girl got it...
Got it honestly
From her mother
Her mother's mother
And then some.

It was her heritage.

Olga Samples Davis

On Opening One Eye

Dear Lord,
                forgive me if I do not wake just yet
although the air unrolls its silk
to ripple in the sunlight wavering through the milk-
gray clouds; although in the lithe grass, all stubby legs,
puppies and kittens tumble, living Easter eggs;
although the morning flows
over my eyelids shut and graceless,
dear Lord, forgive me, if I seek repose
from night, the nurse who, dark and faceless,
lays me on her dry breasts without a song.
I will wake before too long,
and over my lean and Lenten ribs
put on, more delicate than spiders' webs,
dear Lord, Your satin day,
and go my way.

Vassar Miller

Roller Rink

That summer it just appeared,
like a huge canvas butterfly
pinned to McNaughton's field.
All of us half-grown came every day
to watch and try, in love
with unlikely motion, with ourselves
and the obscure brother
who was older and came from a nameless far end
of the county. He knew, from somewhere,
how to do it, the dance of it turning
faster than music, could bend
and glide smooth as a fish where we fell,
could leap, land and roll on
squatting, backward, one-footed.
We loved him for looking blade-boned and frail,
for being always alone with nothing to tell.

In August the old man who'd taken our change
hefted sections of floor and his tent
and his music into a truckbed and left.
The autumn that came after
rose for us with so perfectly clear
a cry of wild geese and amber light
on its early winds, with so many stars
let loose, and leaves in the rain—
even our shambling, hopeless town
seemed good, just in that turn
before the wheel of the year came down.

Of course it never came again.
There was the round brown place
where grass wouldn't grow in that field,
but would grow next year with great ghost wheels
of queen anne's lace.
That summer was a line we'd stumbled over,
and so we were free to fall and gather
the dear, unskillful, amazing losses
departure needs. We took them all,
our bodies shooting crazily
into and through each other. And finally past
to army, city, anyplace far.
We took any road out we could take;
but none of us with the sweet-lifting grace
and ease of the promise that farm boy made
who went and stayed.

Betty Adcock

i need a new prompt

i need a new prompt
the old one is
a grayish cocoon dangling from the eave by the back door
a blackened pecan shell crumbling in the corner of the utility
       room
a wrinkled brown-tipped rose drooping over the edge of the
       driveway
the life is gone
consumed by the barbeque flame
eaten
fast frozen, freeze dried
where is that phoenix fellow when you need him
i need a new prompt

John Eubanks

Cinderella

My step-sisters are willing
to cut off their toes for him.

What would I do for those days
when I played alone
in the hazel tree over my mother's grave?

I would go backwards if I could
and stay in that moment when the doves
fluttered down with the golden gown.

But everything has changed.
I trace his form in the ashes,
and then sweep it away before they see.

He's been on parade with that shoe.
All Prince, with heralds and entourage,
they come trumpeting through the village.

If he found me, would he recognize me,
my face, after mistaking their feet for mine?
I want to crawl away

into my pigeon house, my pear tree.
The world is too large, bright like a ballroom
and then suddenly dark.

Mother, no one prepared me for this—
for the soft heat of a man's neck when he dances
or the thickness of his arms.

Gwen Strauss

Valentine for Ernest Mann

You can't order a poem like you order a taco.
Walk up to the counter, say, "I'll take two"
and expect it to be handed back to you
on a shiny plate.

Still, I like your spirit.
Anyone who says, "Here's my address,
write me a poem," deserves something in reply.
So I'll tell you a secret instead:
poems hide. In the bottoms of our shoes,
they are sleeping. They are the shadows
drifting across our ceilings the moment
before we wake up. What we have to do
is live in a way that lets us find them.

Once I knew a man who gave his wife
two skunks for a valentine.
He couldn't understand why she was crying.
"I thought they had such beautiful eyes."
And he was serious. He was a serious man
who lived in a serious way. Nothing was ugly
just because the world said so. He really
liked those skunks. So, he re-invented them
as valentines and they became beautiful.
At least, to him. And the poems that had been hiding
in the eyes of skunks for centuries
crawled out and curled up at his feet.

Maybe if we re-invent whatever our lives give us
we find poems. Check your garage, the odd sock
in your drawer, the person you almost like, but not quite.
And let me know.

Naomi Shihab Nye

Beverages

Horse by Moonlight

For Juan Soriano

A horse escaped from the circus
and lodged in my daughter's eyes:
there he ran circles around the iris
raising silver dust-clouds in the pupil
and halting sometimes
to drink from the holy water of the retina.

Since then my daughter feels a longing
for meadows of grass and green hills...
waiting for the moon to come
and dry with its silk sleeves
the sad water that wets her cheeks.

Alberto Blanco

Translated by Jennifer Clement

Craft Lost in Texas

The poet and all
six passengers of
a small poetry reading
were lost late last night
when they went into a dive
outside of Houston.

Peter Klappert

Good Water

the cup holds
a ball,
the ball becomes
a skull,
the skull breaks
into matchsticks,
the matchsticks congeal
into gold,
the gold powders
into the dust on a moth's wing,
the moth wing expands
and is a blanket of silk,
the blanket of silk covers a foot,
the foot belongs to someone who
never cuts his toenails,
the long sharp toenails,
like trowels, repel dirt, they
dig into the soil/a man
becomes a garden tool,
the garden tool hangs
in the garage,
the garage is closed for the winter,
winter is full of snow,
the snow melts into water,
the water is in the cup.

Diane Wakoski

Light Snacks

In Praise of ABC

In the beginning were the letters,
wooden, awkward, and everywhere.
Before the Word was the slow scrabble of fire and water.

God bless my son and his wooden letters
who has gone to bed with A in his right hand and Z in his left,
who has walked all day with C in his shoe and said nothing,
who has eaten of his napkin the word Birthday,
and who has filled my house with the broken speech of wizards.

To him the grass makes its gentle sign.
For him the worm letters her gospel truth.
To him the pretzel says, I am the occult
descendant of the first blessed bread
and the lost cuneiform of a grain of wheat.

Kneading bread, I found in my kitchen half an O.
Now I wait for someone to come from far off
holding the other half, saying,
What is broken shall be made whole.
Match half for half; now do you know me again?

Thanks be to God for my house seeded with dark sayings
and my rooms rumpled and badly lit
but richly lettered with the secret raisins of truth.

Nancy Willard

while dissecting frogs in biology class
scrut discovers the intricacies of the
scooped neckline in his lab partner's dress

oh madame curie
oh louis pasteur

oh ponce de leon
and christopher columbus

you have nothing on me today

George Roberts

Spade Scharnweber

Spade Scharnweber was a white Watusi. His mother,
who was an even 5 feet, had nightmares of giving
birth to a foreigner who never stopped unspooling.

And Spade laid two claims to fame.

One, he had to have an extended rod welded to his bike
seat so that when he rode he could keep his knees
out of his salivaries.

But the other was more renown. Spade was the only
letterman who was tall enough to lie across the
ceiling panels from the boy's locker room to where
the girls were dressing.

We held his feet as if they were a witching wand, and
when Spade trembled, we knew his eyes were there.

When his arches inflated, we knew he'd seen Ina Claire
Frischoltz, and for a poor equivalent, he once
showed us one of those girlie cards Eagles used
to carry from their Aerie.

But by the time he was a senior, I guess his mother's
turnips had done their thing. His clavicles
thickened, and his bones grew so heavy they spoke
loads of sand. So we shouldn't have been surprised
when Spade fell through the ceiling tiles one day
and hung like a limp joint over studs that held
two laughing, screaming walls.

As we held his milk-of-magnesia ankles, Miss Charlotte
     Crue, PE teacher and civics coach, slapped his
     face with a virginal towel 7 adolescent light years
     from his toes.

And Ina Claire tells me the hole's still there, that
     Stockville girls still expect a mantis in a maroon
     letter sweater to descend upon them with bug eyes,
     somehow thickening their grace.

Don Welch

The Courtship

When Sickly Jim Wilson's first wife died
he tried to carry on
keep house and farm his scrabbly land
and it like to broke him.
All them kids were too old to stay put
and too young to carry water. There was no one
to cook, wash, or sew, no one but Sickly Jim
and him the same body who must milk the cow
and plant the scanty hay. Soon he saw
he had to have another wife.

He considered the prospects on the creek,
listed them according to his favor:
Widow Jones, Miss Creech, the oldest Phillips girl,
and even Mossie Maggern. The thought of Mossie
made his belly cold, but next morning he set out.

Widow Jones was stringing beans on her hillside
porch. He rode right up to the rail.
"Morning Miz Jones. How are you now?"
"Working steady," was her answer,
"and how about yourself?" "Not faring well,
not faring well at all. If I'm to farm
and raise my kids, I've got to have a helpmeet.
That's why I'm here. It looks to me
like you might be the one. What do you say?"

She studied him, walked to the edge of the porch.
"I didn't think wives were got
the way a man gets pigs or harness.
I thought it usually took a little time
and a feller got off his horse."
"You know, Miz Jones, I mean no offense
but time's a thing I've run short of.
I've got babies crying at home
and so I speak out plain."
"Well give me the day. You come back
around suppertime for my answer."
"No ma'am. I need a wife before that."
He looked at the paper in his hand.
"You're the first on my list, but if you
can't oblige, I'll be off to try Miss Creech."

He settled his hat, turned his horse,
and was almost out of the yard
when she called to him, "I've given it thought.
It's clear I'm the wife you need.
Hold till Sunday and I'll marry you."
And that's just what she did.

George Ella Lyon

Epitaphs

For a Math Student

His days were numbered. Here lies a digital tyro
Totalled, letting X be the unknown,
Cross-multiplying, equating himself with zero,
Learning at length the root of minus one.

For a Comedian

Here lies a stand-up comic, on his first
Unlimited engagement, playing it dead-pan,
Playing it low and blue, under-rehearsed,
With four chiselled one-liners, a straight man.

For a Dog Trainer

He strained at his leash and whined, but Death said, "Heel!"
And he heeled. "Sit!" and he sat. "Stay!" and he stayed.
When Death said, "Come!" he came, obedient, faithful,
Anxious to play. "Play dead!" Death said, and he played.

For a Midget

He knew his life would be short: that's how it began.
Others grew up, but he stayed undersize,
Freaked out in an outsize world, not called a man.
Look down on him now: he was used to downcast eyes.

For a Grammarian

Here, parsed forever in a complete sentence
With no independent clause, with no direct
Object among other neuter pronouns,
Without an active verb, without a subject . . .

For a Nudist

He shed his clothes, believing nothing should lie
Between his skin and the sun. Now nothing does
But grass and dirt and steel and mahogany
And satin and wool and polyester and moss.

David Wagoner

After the Dentist

My left upper
lip and half

my nose is gone.
I drink my coffee

on the right from
a warped cup

whose left lip dips.
My cigarette's

thick as a finger.
Somebody else's.

I put lip-
stick on a cloth-

stuffed doll's
face that's

surprised when one
side smiles.

May Swenson

To a Daughter Leaving Home

When I taught you
at eight to ride
a bicycle, loping along
beside you
as you wobbled away
on two round wheels,
my own mouth rounding
in surprise when you pulled
ahead down the curved
path of the park,
I kept waiting
for the thud
of your crash as I
sprinted to catch up,
while you grew
smaller, more breakable
with distance,
pumping, pumping
for your life, screaming
with laughter,
the hair flapping
behind you like a
handkerchief waving
goodbye.

Linda Pastan

The Unchosen

Yesterday's hard play still clinging
to the smell of T-shirt
brings back the fall of fourth grade
when friends turned into strangers,
and differences became like hairlines on old men.

I remember standing at the edge
of the park near the cedar bush
that had been summer's hideout
and watching as friends double crossed
into the center span of grass
we had avoided all summer long.

There were no trees in that part of the park
—the magic long removed—
the benches moved along the bushes,
silent centennials to organized games.
But the bushes had held Nazis and Nippons,
we strafed them from June into July.

They had needed my clumsiness
to excite what might be in the clumps of bushes
there to the right of swings.
But,this fall game was one I would not be chosen for
—straightforward and agile,
they could play without my imagination.

I stood there long enough for sweat
to begin to shuck their shirts.
Bare chested these summer friends
changed into strangers
who could not, would not ever choose me.

Edward E. Wilson

Repercussion

Mrs. Hilliard dresses her front yard
with a wagon wheel, a longhorn skull
this sophisticated trash heap,
the newest look in lawn care

the neighbors gawk, laugh,
shake their heads, bewildered
their white-tarred trees shine,
and trimmed lawns wink at one another

Before she was mother's enemy,
her daughter baby sat
One night, after my parents returned,
I would not sleep
too afraid of what hides in the darkness of my mind

after prodding out my fears
pleading for my thoughts, Mom heard:
"The monster!"
my shaking fingers produced the picture
fangs dripped saliva
clawed fingers dangle blood
"Mrs. Hilliard drew it, to show me how
when I spit, the monster will come
cut out my tongue."
Mom screamed across the alleyway
You don't scare children to make them mind!

In response a toilet appears
pristine white, to decorate the lawn
drive Mother crazy,
its ugliness somehow
a reflection on her

fake blue flowers, brazen, stick
petals and bulbs above the rim of that pot
peeking at the neighborhood
watching for children who spit
who trespass
kill cats

when her children wail
compassion drowns us
Mother covers my ears
refuses to object
she's worried about a bathtub,
a rusty horseless plow,
or a white water heater,
placed to match the trees,
the pot and the skull.

Mona Robinson

Plain Geometry

> Paradox: Sometimes a
> seemingly sound analysis
> leads to a conclusion that
> contradicts fact.
> Geometry
> Ray Jergensen

The shapes of our lives
don't fit neatly together.

You're rectangles.
        I'm circles.
You organize.
        I fantasize.
Your questions
need answers.
        My answers are
        usually questions.
You move directly
from point A to point B.
        I wander
        within parabolas.
You connect days
in a collinear progression.
        I slip in and out
        of yesterday
        in lazy coplanar patterns.
You deduce pleasure
from the arcs and angles
of our intersecting bodies.
        I tessellate moments
        we steal from the world
        to form our own
        design of passion.

You find strength
in solid proof.
      I find strength
      in you
      and those corners
      of our hearts
      that we share.

Anita Arnold

Old Flame

I never then noticed the rather sausage-like trotters
That toted incomparable glory down the street
Schoolward, for glory's the only thing that matters,
That glory then being twin braids plaited plump and neat,

One over each shoulder with a bewitching twitch
To mark each pace as I followed, drifting, tongue-tied,
Gaze fixed on the sun's stunning paradox which
Gave to blackness a secret flaming that blackness denied.

Tongue-tied—why, yes. And besides, she was somewhat older,
So in nine years no word ever passed, certainly not conversation.
Then I was gone, and as far as I cared, she could moulder,
Braids and all, in the grave, life carved in compressed notation.

A half-century later, stranger on streets back home,
I heard my name, but on turning saw no one I knew.
Then I saw the mouth open and move, of a grisly old dame,
With gingham, false teeth, gray hair, and heard words: "Why,
it's you!"

Well, yes, it was me, but who was that pile of age-litter?
"Don't you know me?" it wailed. Then suddenly, by Christ, I did.
So at last conversation—just factual, not joyous or bitter:
Twice widowed, grandmother, but comfortably fixed, she said,

And solstice and solstice will heave on, on its axis earth grind,
And black Cadillacs scarcely hold a funereal pace.
When her name escapes, I can usually call to mind
Sausage-legs, maybe some kind of braids. Never, never, a face.

Robert Penn Warren

Eleven

And summer mornings the mute child, rebellious,
Stupid, hating the words, the meanings, hating
The Think now, Think, the Oh but Think! would leave
On tiptoe the three chairs on the verandah
And crossing tree by tree the empty lawn
Push back the shed door and upon the sill
Stand pressing out the sunlight from his eyes
And enter and with outstretched fingers feel
The grindstone and behind it the bare wall
And turn and in the corner on the cool
Hard earth sit listening. And one by one,
Out of the dazzled shadow in the room,
The shapes would gather, the brown plowshare, spades,
Mattocks, the polished helves of picks, a scythe
Hung from the rafters, shovels, slender tines
Glinting across the curve of sickles—shapes
Older than men were, the wise tools, the iron
Friendly with earth. And sit there, quiet, breathing
The harsh dry smell of withered bulbs, the faint
Odor of dung, the silence. And outside
Beyond the half-shut door the blind leaves
And the corn moving. And at noon would come,
Up from the garden, his hard crooked hands
Gentle with earth, his knees still earth-stained, smelling
Of sun, of summer, the old gardener, like

A priest, like an interpreter, and bend
Over his baskets.
                    And they would not speak:
They would say nothing. And the child would sit there
Happy as though he had no name, as though
He had been no one: like a leaf, a stem,
Like a root growing—

Archibald MacLeish

Money
an introductory lecture

This morning we shall spend a few minutes
Upon the study of symbolism, which is basic
To the nature of money. I show you this nickel.
Icons and cryptograms are written all over
The nickel: one side shows a hunchbacked bison
Bending his head and curling his tail to accommodate
The circular nature of money. Over him arches
UNITED STATES OF AMERICA, and, squinched in
Between that and his rump, E PLURIBUS UNUM,
A Roman reminiscence that appears to mean
An indeterminately large number of things
All of which are the same. Under the bison
A straight line giving him a ground to stand on
Reads FIVE CENTS. And on the other side of our nickel
There is the profile of a man with long hair
And a couple of feathers in the hair; we know
Somehow that he is an American Indian, and
He wears the number nineteen-thirty-six.
Right in front of his eyes the word LIBERTY, bent
To conform with the curve of the rim, appears
To be falling out of the sky Y first; the Indian
Keeps his eyes downcast and does not notice this;
To notice it, indeed, would be shortsighted of him.
So much for the iconography of one of our nickels,
Which is now becoming a rarity and something of
A collectors' item: for as a matter of fact
There is almost nothing you can buy with a nickel,
The representative American Indian was destroyed
A hundred years or so ago, and his descendants'
Relations with liberty are maintained with reservations,
Or primitive concentration camps; while the bison,
Except for a few examples kept in cages,
Is now extinct. Something like that, I think,
Is what Keats must have meant in his celebrated
Ode on a Grecian Urn.

Notice, in conclusion,
A number of circumstances sometimes overlooked
Even by experts: (*a*) Indian and bison,
Confined to obverse and reverse of the coin,
Can never see each other; (*b*) they are looking
In opposite directions, the bison past
The Indian's feathers, the Indian past
The bison's tail; (*c*) they are upside down
To one another; (*d*) the bison has a human face
Somewhat resembling that of Jupiter Ammon.
I hope that our studies today will have shown you
Something of the import of symbolism
With respect to the understanding of what is symbolized.

Howard Nemerov

What is Supposed to Happen

When you were small,
we watched you sleeping,
waves of breath
filling your chest.
Sometimes we hid behind
the wall of baby, soft cradle
of baby needs.
I loved carrying you between
my own body and the world.

Now you are sharpening pencils,
entering the forest of
lunch boxes, little desks.
People I never saw before
call out your name
and you wave.

This loss I feel,
this shrinking,
as your field of roses
grows and grows....

Now I understand history.
Now I understand my mother's
ancient eyes.

Naomi Shihab Nye

The Myth of Perfectability

I hang the still life of flowers
by a window so it can receive
the morning light, as flowers must.
But sun will fade the paint,
so I move the picture to the exact center
of a dark wall, over the mantel
where it looks too much like a trophy—
one of those animal heads
but made up of blossoms.
I move it again to a little wall
down a hallway where I can come upon it
almost by chance, the way the Japanese
put a small window in an obscure place,
hoping that the sight of a particular landscape
will startle them with beauty as they pass
and not become familiar.
I do this all day long, moving
the picture or sometimes a chair or a vase
from place to place. Or else
I sit here at the typewriter,
putting in a comma to slow down
a long sentence, then taking it out,
then putting it back again
until I feel like a happy Sisyphus,
or like a good farmer who knows
that the body's work is never over,
for the motions of plowing and planting continue
season after season, even in his sleep.

Linda Pastan

Ruby Was Her Name

My mother, who opened my eyes, who
brought me into the terrible world,
was guilty. Her look apologized:
she knew what anyone said was true about us
but therefore unfair. How could they blame us
for doing the things we were set to do?

Never heroic, never a model
for us, or for anyone, she cowered
and looked from the corner of her eye—
"Et tu?" And it always meant we were
with her, alas. No one else
could find the center of the world.

She found the truth like a victim; it hit
her again and again, and she always cried out.
At the end she turned to me, helplessly
honest still: "Oh, Bill, I'm afraid,"
and the whole of her life went back to her heart,
from me in a look for the look she gave.

William Stafford

Sandwiches

For the Departure of a Stepson

You are going for a long time
and nobody knows what to expect

we are trying to learn
not to accompany gifts with advice

or to suppose that we can protect you
from being changed

by something that we do not know
but have always turned away from

even by the sea that we love
with its breaking

and the dissolving days
and the shadows on the wall

together we look at the young trees
we read the news we smell the morning

we cannot tell you what to take with you
in your light baggage

W. S. Merwin

Peace Walk

We wondered what our walk should mean,
taking that un-march quietly;
the sun stared at our signs— "Thou shalt not kill."

Men by a tavern said, "Those foreigners..."
to a woman with a fur, who turned away—
like an elevator going down, their look at us.

Along a curb, their signs lined across,
a picket line stopped and stared
the whole width of the street at ours: "Unfair."

Above our heads the sound truck blared—
by the park, under the autumn trees—
it said that love could fill the atmosphere:

Occur, slow the other fallout, unseen,
on islands everywhere—fallout, falling
unheard. We held our poster up to shade our eyes.

At the end we just walked away;
no one was there to tell us where to leave the signs.

William Stafford

We Used to Play

a game called kick the can, which used to last about a month.
That's how long it took to catch Fred Tooley.

Tooley was a fat kid. He used to pick his nose just after
recess as if he hadn't purged himself enough in soccer.
When the early fall would come in through the window,
cold as a spoon against our cheeks, Tooley would sit
in Math IV eating dirt stewed with asthma.

Miss Johnson said his system was lacking (this was always
after she'd spanked his hands), but his brain wasn't.
Tooley never hid more than 50 yards from the can in
front of Harold's house, and we still spent months
trying to find him. I'll never understand how he got
under the latticed facade of Bonehead Eiler's porch
one time. We found him with Bonehead's dog and 13
pups. He went to hide before she was bred.

As I said, it was just a game, but taken seriously enough
to take to bed. I remember how often I dreamed of
finding Tooley under a pile of leaves in the front
yard, or behind the seat of old man Arnold's tank
truck. I never dreamed of Tooley home in bed.

And I remember walking to school past Jim Hink's house
and wondering if Hink's father had eaten Fred. Old
man Hink was mean. There was this trail across the
backyard where he dragged dead spirit in his foot.
I remember the two lines of dirt and the thin line
of grass which old Hink's insole never touched. He
must have fit his foot to the ruts and ridden bearings
of dirt all the way to the back door. I guess that
was the only place in the neighborhood too narrow
for Fred Tooley.

But when I got to school there he'd be, leaning his fat
against those heavy doors we had to help the kinder-
garteners with. There he'd be, playing the aardvark,
sticking his tongue out, eating those soft beebees
for breakfast, and he'd say, "Wanna play kick the can?"

Don Welch

Cub Scouts and Yellow Corn

We figured they might run out of food
by the time our turn came,
but no, a drumstick and wing, skins
crackling fat, and bright yellow
ear of corn on styrofoam plates.

Award night for the Cubs
at Braun Station Elementary School.
Neckerchiefs folded, sleeves pressed crisp,
the members of Den 4 have earned
their transformations into bears,
Den 6 into wolves, small white teeth
stripping the rows of corn.
The boys have not grown fur, only
tufts of hair that poke
and tangle under their caps.

No more woods in this neighborhood.
The few cedars left will be cut down—
rough, shaggy trees, they don't bend
to garden plans. This past summer
a bobcat came through these hills,
maybe driven down by the drought,
killed a Golden Retriever.

When the last raffle ticket has been drawn
from Frank Vargas' blue and gold cap,
we scrape back our chairs,
drive home in the cold blue night
with our boys who are wolves, who are bears.
We ask if their homework is done
before we make sure the dogs are in,
before we turn out the lights.

We sleep on clean sheets
and dream of corn—fields, miles
of corn, stretching, chattering
under the moon, tassels spilling
feathery, yellow fur.

Wendy Barker

Salads

Love Poem

My clumsiest dear, whose hands shipwreck vases,
At whose quick touch all glasses chip and ring,
Whose palms are bulls in china, burs in linen,
And have no cunning with any soft thing

Except all ill-at-ease fidgeting people:
The refugee uncertain at the door
You make at home; deftly you steady
The drunk clambering on his undulant floor.

Unpredictable dear, the taxi driver's terror,
Shrinking from far headlights pale as a dime
Yet leaping before red apoplectic streetcars—
Misfits in any space. And never on time.

A wrench in clocks and the solar system. Only
With words and people and love you move at ease.
In traffic of wit expertly manoeuvre
And keep us, all devotion, at your knees.

Forgetting your coffee spreading on our flannel,
Your lipstick grinning on our coat,
So gayly in love's unbreakable heaven
Our souls on glory of spilt bourbon float.

Be with me, darling, early and late. Smash glasses—
I will study wry music for your sake.
For should your hands drop white and empty
All the toys of the world would break.

John Frederick Nims

Inside a Poem

It doesn't always have to rhyme,
but there's the repeat of a beat, somewhere
an inner chime that makes you want to
tap your feet or swerve in a curve;
a lilt, a leap, a lightning-split:—
thunderstruck the consonants jut,
while the vowels open wide as waves in the noon-
      blue sea.

Eve Merriam

How to Stuff a Pepper

Now, said the cook, I will teach you
how to stuff a pepper with rice.

Take your pepper green, and gently,
for peppers are shy. No matter which side
you approach, it's always the backside.
Perched on green buttocks, the pepper sleeps.
In its silk tights, it dreams
of somersaults and parsley,
of the days when the sexes were one.

Slash open the sleeve
as if you were cutting a paper lantern,
and enter a moon, spilled like a melon,
a fever of pearls,
a conversation of glaciers.
It is a temple built to the worship
of morning light.

I have sat under the great globe
of seeds on the roof of that chamber,
too dazzled to gather the taste I came for.
I have taken the pepper in hand,
smooth and blind, a runt in the rich
evolution of roses and ferns.
You say I have not yet taught you

to stuff a pepper?
Cooking takes time.

Next time we'll consider the rice.

Nancy Willard

Fifteen

South of the Bridge on Seventeenth
I found back of the willows one summer
day a motorcycle with engine running
as it lay on its side, ticking over
slowly in the high grass. I was fifteen.

I admired all that pulsing gleam, the
shiny flanks, the demure headlights
fringed where it lay; I led it gently
to the road and stood with that
companion, ready and friendly. I was fifteen.

We could find the end of a road, meet
the sky on out Seventeenth. I thought about
hills, and patting the handle got back a
confident opinion. On the bridge we indulged
a forward feeling, a tremble. I was fifteen.

Thinking, back farther in the grass I found
the owner, just coming to, where he had flipped
over the rail. He had blood on his hand, was pale—
I helped him walk to his machine. He ran his hand
over it, called me good man, roared away.

I stood there, fifteen.

William Stafford

The Poet Dreams of a Nice Warm Motel

Of course the plane is late
two hours twisting bumpily
over Chicago in a droning grey funk
with the seatbelt sign on.
Either you are met by seven
young Marxists who want to know
at once What Is To Be Done
or one professor who says, What?
You have luggage. But I
parked in the no
parking zone.

Oh, we wouldn't want to put you
up at a motel, we here at
Southwestern Orthodontic Methodist,
we want you to feel homey:
drafty rooms where icicles
drip on your forehead, dorm cubicles
under the belltower where
the bells boom all night
on each quarter hour, rooms in faculty attics
you share with seven crying
babies with measles, rooms two
miles from a bathroom.
                           The bed
is a quarter inch mattress
flung upon springs of upended
razor blades: the mattress
is stuffed with fingernail
clippings and the feathers of buzzards.
If you roll over or cough it
sounds like a five car collision.

The mattress is shaped that way
because our pet hippo Sweetie
likes to nap there. It's homey,
isn't it, meaning we're going to keep
you up with instant coffee
until two a.m. discussing why
we at Middle Fork State Teachers College
don't think you are truly great.

You'll love our dog Ogre,
she adores sleeping with guests
especially when she's in heat.
Don't worry, the children
will wake you. (They do.)
In the morning while all
fourteen children (the ones
with the flu and whooping cough
and oh, you haven't had
the mumps—I mean, yet?) assault
you with tomahawks and strawberry
jam, you are asked, oh,
would you like breakfast?
Naturally we never eat
breakfast ourselves, we believe
fasting purifies the system.
Have some cold tofu,
don't mind the mold.

No, we didn't order
your books, that's rampant
commercialism. We will call you
Miz Percy and make a joke about
women's libbers. The mike was run
over by a snowplow.
If we were too busy to put
up posters, we've obtained the

outdoor Greek Amphitheater
where you'll read to me and my wife.
If we blanketed five states
with announcements, we will be astounded
when five hundred cram into
the women's restroom we reserved.

Oh yes, the check will be four
months late. The next hungry poet
will be told, you'll be real comfortable
here, What's-her-name, she wrote that book
The Flying Dyke, she was through last year
and she found it real homey
in the Athens of the West.

Marge Piercy

Two Friends

I have something to tell you.
I'm listening.
I'm dying.
I'm sorry to hear.
I'm growing old.
It's terrible.
It is, I thought you should know.
Of course and I'm sorry. Keep in touch.
I will and you too.
And let me know what's new.
Certainly, though it can't be much.
And stay well.
And you too.
And go slow.
And you too.

David Ignatow

Daily Specials

The Road Not Taken

Two roads diverged in a yellow wood,
And sorry I could not travel both
And be one traveler, long I stood
And looked down one as far as I could
To where it bent in the undergrowth;

Then took the other, as just as fair,
And having perhaps the better claim,
Because it was grassy and wanted wear;
Though as for that, the passing there
Had worn them really about the same,

And both that morning equally lay
In leaves no step had trodden black.
Oh, I kept the first for another day!
Yet knowing how way leads on to way,
I doubted if I should ever come back.

I shall be telling this with a sigh
Somewhere ages and ages hence:
Two roads diverged in a wood, and I—
I took the one less traveled by,
And that has made all the difference.

Robert Frost

Saying Yes

"Are you Chinese?"
"Yes."

"American?"
"Yes."

"*Really* Chinese?"
"No...not quite."

"*Really* American?"
"Well, actually, you see..."

But I would rather say
yes

Not neither-nor,
not maybe,
but both, and not only

The homes I've had,
the ways I am

I'd rather say it
twice,
yes

Diana Chang

Ode to My Southern Drawl

Here in the south
my tongue relaxes
under the warm blanket of my language.

I've been away too long
in places where tongues are clipped
and I must say
if I may
I'm happier here
where dogs are named Duke
because they're redbones
and our sons have soft names
like Hampton and Buddy
There aren't any blizzards in *y'all*

and even though the
temperatures may drop
the name is *blue norther*
not *coldsnap*
which is too abrupt.
I used to blush at my maiden tongue
my badge of ignorance
my scarlet letter among the *literati*.
But not any more.
And I like it when my friends
say "G I R L!" in a whole note
whenever I bring them a casserole
for no other reason
than casserole feels good to say.

I know it's heat
at the root of my southern drawl.
I know this
because in cold climates
you cannot speak slowly
or your teeth will clamp down
onto your tongue and punish it
for leaving your mouth open so long.
You have to spit out the words
or else biting air will slip
between your lips
and strangle you.

No, no
in the north
there's no relishing
                no pondering
                        no savoring
a particular turn of phrase
no allowing the l's to roll   roll   roll
across the soft palate.

Here in the south
we treat words like wine
letting them rest in our mouths
until they are ripe and
have soaked into the sides of our cheeks.
And sometimes they get so warm,
we have to cool them
off with iced tea
or Coca Cola

        or else we change the subject

which could be anything

from husbands
to the gospel
to the PTA
and if we talk gospel
well, we always choose Luke
because Luke feels so good
up against the back of our throats.
And honey,
why not let the message
go ahead and give us a little massage?
        I mean
isn't that what the good Lord intended
when he said,
First, *there was the word*?

Kathi Appelt

Painting the Gate

I painted the mailbox. That was fun.
I painted it postal blue.
Then I painted the gate.
I painted a spider that got on the gate.
I painted his mate.
I painted the ivy around the gate.
Some stones I painted blue,
and part of the cat as he rubbed by.
I painted my hair. I painted my shoe.
I painted the slats, both front and back,
all their beveled edges, too.
I painted the numbers on the gate—
I shouldn't have, but it was too late.
I painted the posts, each side and top,
I painted the hinges, the handle, the lock,
several ants and a moth asleep in a crack.
At last I was through.
I'd painted the gate
shut, me out, with both hands dark blue,
as well as my nose, which,
early on, because of a sudden itch,
got painted. But wait!
I had painted the gate.

May Swenson

"Out, Out—"

The buzz saw snarled and rattled in the yard
And made dust and dropped stove-length sticks of wood,
Sweet-scented stuff when the breeze drew across it.
And from there those that lifted eyes could count
Five mountain ranges one behind the other
Under the sunset far into Vermont.
And the saw snarled and rattled, snarled and rattled,
As it ran light, or had to bear a load.
And nothing happened: day was all but done.
Call it a day, I wish they might have said
To please the boy by giving him the half hour
That a boy counts so much when saved from work.
His sister stood beside them in her apron
To tell them 'Supper.' At the word, the saw,
As if to prove saws knew what supper meant,
Leaped out at the boy's hand, or seemed to leap—
He must have given the hand. However it was,
Neither refused the meeting. But the hand!
The boy's first outcry was a rueful laugh,
As he swung toward them holding up the hand,
Half in appeal, but half as if to keep
The life from spilling. Then the boy saw all—
Since he was old enough to know, big boy
Doing a man's work, though a child at heart—
He saw all spoiled. 'Don't let him cut my hand off—
The doctor, when he comes. Don't let him, sister!'
So. But the hand was gone already.
The doctor put him in the dark of ether.
He lay and puffed his lips out with his breath.
And then—the watcher at his pulse took fright.
No one believed. They listened at his heart.
Little—less—nothing!—and that ended it.
No more to build on there. And they, since they
Were not the one dead, turned to their affairs.

Robert Frost

All That Time

I saw two trees embracing.
One leaned on the other
as if to throw her down.
But she was the upright one.
Since their twin youth, maybe she
had been pulling him toward her
all that time,

and finally almost uproooted him.
He was the thin, dry, insecure one,
the most wind-warped, you could see.
And where their tops tangled
it looked like he was crying
on her shoulder.
On the other hand, maybe he

had been trying to weaken her,
break her, or at least
make her bend
over backwards for him
just a little bit.
And all that time
she was standing up to him

the best she could.
She was the most stubborn,
the straightest one, that's a fact.
But he had been willing
to change himself--
even if it was for the worse--
all that time.

At the top they looked like one
tree, where they were embracing.
It was plain they'd be
always together.
Too late now to part.
When the wind blew, you could hear
them rubbing on each other.

May Swenson

An Old Man's Passing

He knew he was old, had known for seven years,
ever since the night Louise walked in from the kitchen,
the mismatched plates and ice tea glasses
shining in the cupboard his mother gave them
when they married, walked into the parlor where he sat
with the *Wood County Democrat* and the checkerboard.
She pulled a rocker to the window and stared across the fields,
the moon full enough to see the wisps of heat
rising from the fresh-plowed earth, and never answered
when he asked if she wanted reds or blacks.
The doctor said it was a stroke—didn't feel a thing,
no more pain than a white-faced cow
when the hammer falls, maybe a vision of stars.

After the funeral, he began to live alone,
something he never planned on doing.
Everybody knew men died first, women were stronger,
more able to fill their days, ignore the past.
He had tried for seven years and only come to understand
that he was old and that an old man alone trying
to keep a hundred-acre farm from turning back to forest
was a paltry thing and must have more sins than he remembered.
Each night he read in the rocker, occasionally looking up.
All he saw was a farmer, his face
a shadow in the window.

He wondered what he looked like now,
bones spilled across the bathroom floor.
Did he catch his foot on the tub,
the bath mat scoot across the tile?
The right knee could have quit for good,
seventy-two years of friction,
nothing left but meal. He knew the hip had broken
when he hit the floor, his by right
of living past allotted time, old folks' greatest fear,
especially those alone and fifteen miles from town.

His head felt like a melon in the August sun.
He closed his eyes, decided he was not afraid,
just embarrassed by this possibly final
resting place. He tried to rise
then told himself to wait.
Louise had always said, "Have faith.
This, too, will pass."
What if no one found him for a week, a month?
They'd burn the house to kill the stink,
let the forest take the fields. He tried again.

At least he wasn't in an Old Folks Home.
Charles Sanders' boys dragged their daddy from the farm,
arthritic fingers curled like a harrow's blades
tearing through soil. If he could only
raise himself, crawl to the bed, pull off the quilt.
This was no way for a man to be found,
not one who even his closest friends called *mister*,
their idea, not his. What if he'd been sitting on the toilet?
He recollected hearing of a woman died that way,
set two days and wouldn't fit a casket.
Nothing but jokes could come of that.

He was amazed he felt no pain, only a slight thirst
he knew would get worse. He tried not to think about it,
choosing instead to dream of wolves,
counting them like sheep, not floating above a fence,
but coming like metal targets at a carnival,
clicking into range from right to left,
tracking across his field, dropping quickly out of sight
to circle underneath, rise again.

When he was young, this country had been full of wolves.
He never understood how they got to East Texas.
Its pines and rolling hills of oak and sweetgum,
its plump cottontails, corn-fed deer

inappropriate for wolves. They needed snow, ancient forests.
They should run in packs, be hungry all the time
and fear no man. Here they always seemed to be in pairs,
male and female, sometimes with pups clumsy at their heels.
He never saw one near the house. They were private animals.
The state offered a bounty for their ears, five dollars a pair.
The carcasses started showing up, wired head down
from fences, tongues dripping between their teeth,
rotting quickly in the humid air.

He swore he'd take no part and made it known
that any wolfer sneaking around his place
might find *himself* dangling from a post.
So it was good he never saw the men who brought the traps,
especially on the day he found the female caught,
her fore-paw broken hard, the bone sticking through.
The male paced at her side.
This was the day after the baby died,
lungs closed tight as little fists.
It was a boy. He tried not think of it
as he held Louise's hand, explained
the nurse would not be bringing the child.
The delivery had been long. Louise could barely talk,
would only sob against his chest. He sat with her
all day and the first night, then said
he had to go to the farm, check the cows.
He'd be back soon. She told him she was alright now.
It was God's will. The Lord would see her through.
She told him she had prayed for him as well.
He thanked her, kissed her cheek, then drove to the farm,
got the rifle and walked the fields.
He couldn't recall why he'd taken the gun,
did not remember wanting to kill anything
and needed no protection.

The wolves were just inside the pines,
south edge of the potato patch.
The female lay on her side, her fur wet.
The big grey male turned toward him, showed this teeth
but made no move to leave his mate.
He remembered stopping a hundred feet away,
sighting the rifle between the yellow eyes.
The wolf dropped without a sound.
When he placed the barrel against the female's ear,
she growled a little and then lay still.
He walked back to the house and got the shovel.
The hole was deep. He dropped them side by side.

It was dark now. He would settle for a drink of water.
He felt no pain. For a moment he wished he had a pistol
but knew he wouldn't use it. Louise would disapprove.
Folks would say he couldn't take it at the end.
That first year after she died, he thought
about the gun, surprised how easy it came.
He also considered selling the place, but where would he go?
Here was something to do. Louise was in every room.

It had all come down to this—an old man
naked on the bathroom floor, lying in his own fluids.
He had never been a man to pray
but he could wait, try to think of pleasant things—
a family of wolves gliding along the distant edges
of a field, a man and a woman
sitting down to checkers after supper.

Robert A. Fink

About Marriage

Don't lock me in wedlock, I want
marriage, an
encounter—

I told you about the
green light of
May

      (a veil of quiet befallen
      the downtown park,
      late

      Saturday after
      noon, long
      shadows and cool

      air, scent of
      new grass,
      fresh leaves,

      blossom on the threshold of
      abundance—

      and the birds I met there,
      birds of passage breaking their journey,
      three birds each of a different species:

      the azalea-breasted with round poll, dark,
      the brindled, merry, mousegliding one,
      and the smallest, golden as gorse and wearing
      a black Venetian mask

      and with them the three douce hen-birds
      feathered in tender, lively brown—

I stood
a half-hour under the enchantment,
no-one passed near,
the birds saw me and

let me be
near them.)
It's not
irrelevant:
I would be
met

and meet you
so,
in a green

airy space, not
locked in.

Denise Levertov

Another Mystery

That time I tagged along with my dad to the dry cleaners—
What'd I know then about Death? Dad comes out carrying
a black suit in a plastic bag. Hangs it up behind the back seat
of the old coupe and says, "This is the suit your grandpa
is going to leave the world in." What on earth
could he be talking about? I wondered.
I touched the plastic, the slippery lapel of that coat
that was going away, along with my grandpa. Those days it was
just another mystery.

Then there was a long interval, a time in which relatives departed
this way and that, left and right. Then it was my dad's turn.
I sat and watched him rise up in his own smoke. He didn't own
a suit. So they dressed him gruesomely
in a cheap sports coat and tie,
for the occasion. Wired his lips
into a smile as if he wanted reassure us, *Don't worry, it's
not as bad as it looks*. But we knew better. He was dead,
wasn't he? What else could go wrong? (His eyelids
were sewn closed, too, so he wouldn't have to witness
the frightful exhibit.) I touched
his hand. Cold. The cheek where a little stubble had
broken through along the jaw. Cold.

Today I reeled this clutter up from the depths.
Just an hour or so ago when I picked up my own suit
from the dry cleaners and hung it carefully behind the back seat.
I drove it home, opened the car door and
lifted it out into sunlight. I stood there a minute
in the road, my fingers crimped on the wire hanger. Then
tore a hole through the plastic to the other side. Took one of
the empty sleeves between my fingers and held it—
the rough, palpable fabric.
I reached through to the other side.

Raymond Carver

Dog's Death

She must have been kicked unseen or brushed by a car.
Too young to know much, she was beginning to learn
To use the newspapers spread on the kitchen floor
And to win, wetting there, the words, "Good dog!
                                        Good dog!"

We thought her shy malaise was a shot reaction.
The autopsy disclosed a rupture in her liver.
As we teased her with play, blood was filling her skin
And her heart was learning to lie down forever.

Monday morning, as the children were noisily fed
And sent to school, she crawled beneath the youngest's bed.
We found her twisted and limp but still alive.
In the car to the vet's, on my lap, she tried

To bite my hand and died. I stroked her warm fur
And my wife called in a voice imperious with tears.
Though surrounded by love that would have upheld her,
Nevertheless she sank and, stiffening, disappeared.

Back home, we found that in the night her frame,
Drawing near to dissolution, had endured the shame
Of diarrhoea and had dragged across the floor
To a newspaper carelessly left there. *Good dog.*

John Updike

At the Piano

One night two hunters, drunk, came in the tent.
They fired their guns and stood there stupidly
as Daddy left the pulpit, stalked toward them,
and slapped them each across the mouth. He split
one's upper lip.
                They beat him like a dog.
They propped their guns against the center pole,
rolled up their sleeves as Daddy stood and preached
about the desecration of God's house.
They punched him down, took turns kicking his ribs,
while thirty old women and sixteen men
sat slack-jawed in their folding chairs and watched.
Just twelve, not knowing what to do, I launched
into "Amazing Grace"—the only hymn
I knew by heart — and everybody sang.
We sang until the hunters grew ashamed
— or maybe tired — and left, taking their guns,
their faces red and gleaming from the work.

They got three years suspended sentence each
and Daddy got another tale of how
Christians are saints and strangers in the world.
I guess he knows. He said that I'd done right
to play the song. God's music saved his life.
But I don't know. I couldn't make a guess.
Can you imagine what it means to be
just barely twelve, a Christian and a girl,
and see your father beaten to a pulp?
Neither can I, God knows, and I was there
in the hot tent, beneath the mildewed cloth,
breathing the August, Alabama air,
and I don't know what happened there, to me.
I told this to my second husband, Jim.
We were just dating then. I cried a lot.
He said, *Hush, dear, at least your father got
a chance to turn all four of his cheeks.*

I laughed. I knew, right then, I was in love.
But still I see that image of my father,
his weight humped on his shoulders as he tried
to stand, and I kept plunging through the song
so I could watch my hands and not his face,
which was rouged crimson with red clay and blood.

Andrew Hudgins

Virgin Mother

within my virgin hand
your kiss in bloom
came to nestle

in my bosom, your son
—my arms
of a madonna
upon my lap maternal
to sleep
I lulled you both

and whoever presumes to judge me
was not born
a child of God

Angela de Hoyos

Gravy

No other word will do. For that's what it was. Gravy.
Gravy, these past ten years.
Alive, sober, working, loving and
being loved by a good woman. Eleven years
ago he was told he had six months to live
at the rate he was going. And he was going
nowhere but down. So he changed his ways
somehow. He quit drinking! And the rest?
After that it was *all* gravy, every minute
of it, up to and including when he was told about,
well, some things that were breaking down and
building up inside his head. "Don't weep for me,"
he said to his friends. "I'm a lucky man.
I've had ten years longer than I or anyone
expected. Pure gravy. And don't forget it."

Raymond Carver

Flight 502
Departing at Gate 23

Waves of heat
writhe on the tarmac.
A platoon of pine boxes
stand at parade rest
obeying orders
one last time.
Smells of strangers,
leis, and suntan lotion
cling to the air I breathe
triggering
silent
  waterfalls
    of memory.

      roadside stands
      where you bought
      pineapple slices
      so fresh the juices
      ran down my sunburned chin

      hiking trips
      into the rainbows
      on Mauna Loa

      bright hibiscus in our hair
      black lava sands
      between our toes

      bruised ribs and coral cuts
      from surfboard runs
      at Makaha

the hectic Honolulu
market place where
you haggled over
cheap beads to slide
between my breasts

pounding surf
playful in the sun
erotic in the salty night

plumeria petals
in our bed
that last weekend
before your air strikes
resumed near Hanoi

But here
now
only cold blue bitterness
wraps its arms around me
and I repeat the litany
of well-meaning friends

You have to go on living
You have to go on living

why

didn't you

Anita Arnold

For You, Who Didn't Know

At four A.M. I dreamed myself on that beach
where we'll take you after you're born.
I woke in a wave of blood.

Lying in the back seat of a nervous Chevy
I counted the traffic lights, lonely as planets.
Starlings stirred in the robes of Justice

over the Town Hall. Miscarriage of justice,
they sang, while you, my small client,
went curling away like smoke under my ribs.

Kick me! I pleaded. Give me a sign
that you're still there!
Train tracks shook our flesh from our bones.

Behind the hospital rose a tree of heaven.
     You can learn something from everything,
     a rabbi told his Hasidim who did not believe it.

     I didn't believe it, either. O rabbi,
     what did you learn on the train to Belsen?
     That because of one second one can miss everything.

There are rooms on this earth for emergencies.
A sleepy attendant steals my clothes and my name,
and leaves me among the sinks on an altar of fear.

"Your name. Your name. Sign these papers,
authorizing us in our wisdom to save the child.
Sign here for circumcision. Your faith, your faith."

     O rabbi, what can we learn from the telegraph?
     asked the Hasidim, who did not understand.
     And he answered, *That every word is counted and charged.*

"This is called a dobtone," smiles the doctor.
He greases my belly, stretched like a drum,
and plants a microphone there, like a flag.

A thousand thumping rabbits! Savages clapping for joy!
A heart dancing its name, I'm here, I'm here!
The cries of fishes, of stars, the tunings of hair!

O rabbi, what can we learn from a telephone?
My shiksa daughter, your faith, your faith
that what we say here is heard there.

Nancy Willard

This Spanish Town

The children are playing
in your ears, old man, your ears
like heels of clay from the arena
of the bull.
Your eyes, old man,
like bronze nails dug
from the boot of a dead matador.

This Spanish town
where mosquitoes hunt
in the jammed aqueducts
whose white columns are bloated
like the bodies of the border guards.

Once there were whispers
and wings in your dreams, pacing
the streets like a hawk who flew
low as the eyes behind cracked shutters.

one flight up. Now you sleep
beneath a child's hat, the shadows
Only of burnt bottles
Beneath you on this street each evening.

Red in dark ashes
Like the eyes
Of the daughter sent
To bring you home
Again tonight.

Jim Carroll

Last Words

Three days ago, my suitcases
were hunched there, in his hospital room,
in the corner, I had to pick them up
by the scruff of their necks, and leave him. I kept
putting them down, and going back
to kiss him again although he was exhausted,
shining like tarnished silver, and yet
I could not seem to pick up those bags
and walk out the door the last time. I kept
going back to the mouth he would lift, his
forehead glittering with effort, his eyes
slewing back, shying, until
finally he cried out *Last kiss!*
and I kissed him and left. This morning, his wife
called to tell me he has ceased to speak,
so those are his last words to me,
the ones he is leaving me with—and it is ending with a *kiss*—
a command for mercy, the offer of his cracked
creator lips. To plead that I leave,
my father asked me for a kiss! I would not
leave till he had done so, I will not let thee go except thou beg for
it.

Sharon Olds

He Makes a House Call

Six, seven years ago
when you began to begin to faint
I painted your leg with iodine

threaded the artery
with the needle and then the tube
pumped your heart with dye enough

to see the valve
almost closed with stone.
We were both under pressure.

Today, in your garden,
kneeling under the sticky fig tree
for tomatoes

I keep remembering your blood.
Seven, it was. I was just
beginning to learn the heart

inside out.
Afterward, your surgery
and the precise valve of steel

and plastic that still pops and clicks
inside like a ping-pong ball.
I should try

chewing tobacco sometimes
if only to see how it tastes.
There is a trace of it at the corner

of your leathery smile
which insists that I see inside
the house: someone named Bill I'm supposed
to know; the royal plastic soldier
whose body fills with whiskey
and marches on a music box

How Dry I Am;
the illuminated 3-D Christ who turns
into Mary from different angles;

the watery basement,
the pills you take, the ivy
that may grow around the ceiling

if it must. Here, you
are in charge—of figs, beans,
tomatoes, life.

At the hospital, a thousand times
I have heard your heart valve open, close.
I know how clumsy it is.

But health is whatever works
and for as long. I keep thinking
of seven years without a faint

on my way to the car
loaded with vegetables
I keep thinking of seven years ago

when you bled in my hands like a saint.

John Stone

Shuttle

She is making stuffing for the turkey;
a few pistachio shells are on the kitchen table.
He looks out the window at the thermometer,

but sees a winter melon with a white glaze
in a New York Chinatown store at night.
Large sea bass swim in a tank by the window;

there are delicate blue crabs in a can
climbing and climbing on each other to get out.
She is thinking of a tapestry of red horses

running across a Southwestern landscape
with blue mesas in the distance. A shuttle goes
back and forth, back and forth through

the different sheds. He is talking to a man
who photographs empty parks in New York,
sees the branches of a black magnolia in early December.

She is washing out yarn so it will pack
and cover the warp; perhaps the tension
isn't right; the texture of Churro fleece

makes her hands tingle; a pot of walnuts
boils on the stove. He turns on the radio,
and listening to Nigerian music

feels the rumble of a subway under the floor,
feels the warmth of his hands
as he watches the snow fall and fall.

Arthur Sze

My Mother Makes a Metaphor

She stretches her hands
across the table
palms down.
They waver, land heavily.
"My hands are wooden," she says.
As if to prove her words,
as if proof were needed,
she picks one up with effort
tries to flex her fingers.
They, like five soldiers, remain rigid.

I see what she means.
Wooden hands cannot plait hair
into thick braids
tie sashes
into balanced bows
feel foreheads
for hot fevers
soothe sorrows.

But wood burns
that is all the meaning I need.
So I reach for her hands
encircle them in mine
understanding in that moment
everything about myself
I never understood before
and nothing about a world
without those beloved hands.

Joyce Armstrong Carroll

Snow White's Father's Second Wife's Tale

The stories leave out the fact
that Snow White's mother and I
were sisters. That when she died
her husband the King
and I both wept.

I had never thought about
which of us was the more beautiful,
it was always the two of us, riding
bareback over the fields,
she would cling to me,

her white breath on my neck.
We thought we were lucky:
two princes, one
for each. But our husbands
were different as snow, fire,

and roses—white roses,
red. I still miss him. Running
through wide fields, the tall
grasses whispering
over our legs—midnights

on a blanket in the forest, the moon
pulling us, reflecting us,
until there was nothing we didn't
know about each other,
until we forgot who was who.

They never told me how he died.
My sister's child came,
white as new sheets,
and then my sister died.
I don't know why

the King insisted we marry—
he wouldn't lie with me
outside in the night,
he said the leaves were damp,
the moss would stain. Why couldn't

I lie still in the pillows?
He stopped coming to me altogether.
I moved into the tower.
I am what happens
when you don't die young.

Wendy Barker

The Forsaken

I

Once in the winter
Out on a lake
In the heart of the north-land,
Far from the Fort
And far from the hunters,
A Chippewa woman
With her sick baby,
Crouched in the last hours
Of a great storm.
Frozen and hungry,
She fished through the ice
With a line of the twisted
Bark of the cedar,
And a rabbit-bone hook
Polished and barbed;
Fished with the bare hook
All through the wild day,
Fished and caught nothing;
While the young chieftain
Tugged at her breasts,
Or slept in the lacing
Of the warm tikanagan.
All the lake surface
Streamed with the hissing
Of millions of iceflakes
Hurled by the wind;
Behind her the round
Of a lonely island
Roared like a fire
With the voice of the storm
In the deeps of the cedars.
Valiant, unshaken,
She took of her own flesh,
Baited the fishhook,
Drew in a gray trout,

Drew in his fellows,
Heaped them beside her,
Dead in the snow.
Valiant, unshaken,
She faced the long distance,
Wolf-haunted and lonely,
Sure of her goal
And the life of her dear one:
Tramped for two days,
On the third in the morning,
Saw the strong bulk
Of the Fort by the river,
Saw the wood smoke
Hang soft in the spruces,
Heard the keen yelp
Of the ravenous huskies
Fighting for whitefish:
Then she had rest.

II

Years and years after,
When she was old and withered,
When her son was an old man
And his children filled with vigor,
They came in their northern tour on the verge of winter,
To an island in a lonely lake.
There one night they camped, and on the morrow
Gathered their kettles and birch bark,
Their rabbit-skin robes and their mink traps,
Launched their canoes and slunk away
        through the islands,
Left her alone forever,
Without a word of farewell,
Because she was old and useless,
Like a paddle broken and warped,
Or a pole that was splintered.

Then, without a sigh,
Valiant, unshaken,
She smoothed her dark locks under her kerchief,
Composed her shawl in state,
Then folded her hands ridged with sinews
            and corded with veins,
Folded them across her breasts spent
            with the nourishing of children,
Gazed at the sky past the tops of the cedars,
Saw two spangled nights arise out of the twilight,
Saw two days go by filled
            with the tranquil sunshine,
Saw, without pain, or dread, or even
            a moment of longing:
Then on the third great night there came
            thronging and thronging
Millions of snowflakes out of a windless cloud;
They covered her close with a beautiful
            crystal shroud,
Covered her deep and silent.
But in the frost of the dawn,
Up from the life below,
Rose a column of breath
Through a tiny cleft in the snow,
Fragile, delicately drawn,
Wavering with its own weakness,
In the wilderness a sign of the spirit,
Persisting still in the sight of the sun
Till day was done.
Then all light was gathered up by the hand of God
            and hid in His breast,
Then there was born a silence deeper than silence,
Then she had rest.

Duncan Campbell Scott

The Whipping

The old woman across the way
        is whipping the boy again
and shouting to the neighborhood
        her goodness and his wrongs.

Wildly he crashes through elephant ears,
        pleads in dusty zinnias,
while she in spite of crippling fat
        pursues and corners him.

She strikes and strikes the shrilly circling
        boy till the stick breaks
in her hand. Her tears are rainy weather
        to woundlike memories:

My head gripped in bony vise
        of knees, the writhing struggle
to wrench free, the blows, the fear
        worse than blows that hateful

Words could bring, the face that I
        no longer knew or loved...
Well, it is over now, it is over,
        and the boy sobs in his room,

And the woman leans muttering against
        a tree, exhausted, purged—
avenged in part for lifelong hidings
        she has had to bear.

Robert Hayden

The .38

I hear the man downstairs slapping the hell out of his
        adulteress wife again
I hear him push and shove her around the overcrowded room
I hear his wife scream and beg for mercy
I hear him tell her there is no mercy
I hear the blows as they land on her beautiful body
I hear glasses and pots and pans falling
I hear her fleeing from the room
I hear them running up the stairs
I hear her outside my door
I hear him coming toward her outside my door
I hear her banging on my door
I hear him bang her head on my door
I hear him trying to drag her away from my door
I hear her hands desperate on my doorknob
I hear the blows of her head against my door
I hear him drag her down the stairs
I hear her head bounce from step to step
I hear them again in their room
I hear a loud smack across her face (I guess)
I hear her groan — then
I hear the eerie silence
I hear him open the top drawer of his bureau (the .38 lives there)
I hear the fast beat of my heart
I hear the drops of perspiration fall from my brow
I hear him yell I warned you
I hear him say damn you I warned you and now it's too late
I hear the loud report of the thirty eight caliber revolver then
I hear it again and again the Smith and Wesson
I hear the bang bang bang of four death dealing bullets
I hear my heart beat faster and louder—then again
I hear the eerie silence
I hear him walk out of their overcrowded room
I hear him walk up the steps
I hear him come toward my door

I hear his hand on the doorknob
I hear the doorknob click
I hear the door slowly open
I hear him step into my room
I hear the click of the thirty eight before the firing pin hits the bullet
I hear the loud blast of the powder exploding in the chamber of the .38
I hear the heavy lead nose of the bullet swiftly cutting its way
        through the barrel of the .38
I hear it emerge into space from the .38
I hear the bullet of death flying toward my head the .38
I hear it coming faster than sound the .38
I hear it coming closer to my sweaty forehead the .38
I hear its weird whistle the .38
I hear it give off a steamlike noise when it cuts through my sweat
        the .38
I hear it singe my skin as it enters my head the .38 and
I hear death saying, *Hello, I'm here!*

Ted Joans

the dream before the last dream

I was on the beach
A smoke of people
Mostly watching
Mostly mute.
Fathers in bathing suits
Holding children in their arms
As if to watch a parade or brushfire
I stood among them but separate
My son was somewhere near me
Idontknowwhereidontknowwhere
But he felt safe to me

The sea was mounting a swift, terrible tumor
Like precision dancers we moved back
The wave dangled to plunge.
Suddenly out of the point in the pull
Where the ocean sucks up its strength
He appeared
He carried one daughter
Like a limp raincoat under his arm
She faced upward
Her back was semicircled and low
Her head dropped
And her hair dragged like a carcass of seaweed
Hehadheratleasthehadher

But where was Corinne
He looked bewildered
But I could not yell to him
He stood a single 8 millimeter frame
But I could not yell to him
He must have thought she was safe with me
Didn't he know he had to go back for Corinne
Atleasthehadtotry
Even though I knew she was safe
Thrashing
In the salt undertow
Somewhere
She had to be
In the waters dark as Welsh slate

Alice Glarden Brand

Revival Week

Buffalo grass had just started to bloom
when Brother Hadley double chinned the announcement
of a one week revival where all sour souls
would be held to the fire, burning, burning—
seven days of sulfurous recriminations at breakfast
made by the Methodist men—seven nights of
altar calls with verses running out
while the minister from down the road
told us, wide-eyed, "Now I'm going to ask
the organist to continue playing *Just As I Am*.
While she plays, I want you to listen to your heart.
There's someone here hurting, Lord, waiting
to come to you, Lord." He'd carry on
for five more verses alternately talking to us
and the Lord.

It was mercy I prayed for, mercy to please send
some sinner down so he could have his soul.
The minister held his Bible with notches
cut out for each soul saved, "Right here
on the Lord's very own book" waving it at us.
He wanted one more notch.
I looked around and thought he preached
to the saved. Everyone in our small congregation
had been revived for every summer since I was six,
at sixteen I could not find any fallen.
We had no visitors who might be pagans
in need of the Lord's mercy.

So after three more verses, I made up my mind
he'd have his notch. Making my way
to the aisle, Brother Hadley said, 'Hallelujah."
Kneeling before his puffy face, I whispered
into his ear, "I didn't think anyone else
was ready to commit, and I'm getting tired.
Tomorrow's geometry test waits me at home,
and I do need to work on proofs, one more time."

Brother Hadley leaned back, raised his eyes,
hands, and voice to the heavens. "The Lord knows
why this young soul came here today. Let us pray."

It was our last revival. Brother Hadley committed suicide
the next spring before the brain tumor forgot his favorite verses.
He did his best to revive us as sinners and saints, and the
tests to come, like the proof of a circle, go on and on.

Edward E. Wilson

Children's Menu

Little Abigail and the Beautiful Pony

There was a girl named Abigail
Who was taking a drive
Through the country
With her parents
When she spied a beautiful sad-eyed
Grey and white pony.
And next to it was a sign
That said,
FOR SALE—CHEAP.
"Oh," said Abigail,
"May I have that pony?
May I please?"
And her parents said,
"No you may not."
And Abigail said,
"But I MUST have that pony."
And her parents said,
"Well, you can't have that pony,
But you can have a nice butter pecan
Ice cream cone when we get home."
And Abigail said,
"I don't want a butter pecan
Ice cream cone.
I WANT THAT PONY—
I MUST HAVE THAT PONY."
And her parents said,
"Be quiet and stop nagging—
You're not getting that pony."
And Abigail began to cry and said,
"If I don't get that pony I'll die.
And her parents said, "You won't die.
No child ever died yet from not getting a pony."
And Abigail felt so bad
That when they got home she went to bed,
And she couldn't eat,
And she couldn't sleep,

And her heart was broken,
And she DID die--
All because of a pony
That her parents wouldn't buy.

(This is a good story
To read to your folks
When they won't buy
You something you want.)

Shel Silverstein

Questions My Son Asked Me, Answers I Never Gave Him

1. Do gorillas have birthdays?
   Yes. Like the rainbow, they happen.
   Like the air, they are not observed.

2. Do butterflies make a noise?
   The wire in the butterfly's tongue
   hums gold.
   Some men hear butterflies
   even in winter.

3. Are they part of our family?
   They forgot us, who forgot how to fly.

4. Who tied my navel? Did God tie it?
   God made the thread: O man, live forever!
   Man made the knot: enough is enough.

5. If I drop my tooth in the telephone
   will it go through the wires and bite someone's ear?
   I have seen earlobes pierced by a tooth of steel.
   It loves what lasts.
   It does not love flesh.
   It leaves a ring of gold in the wound.

6. If I stand on my head
   will the sleep in my eye roll up into my head?
   Does the dream know its own father?
   Can bread go back to the field of its birth?

7. Can I eat a star?
   Yes, with the mouth of time
   that enjoys everything.

8. Could we Xerox the moon?
    This is the first commandment:
    I am the moon, thy moon.
    Thou shalt have no other moons before thee.

9. Who invented water?
    The hands of the air, that wanted to wash each other.

10. What happens at the end of numbers?
    I see three men running toward a field.
    At the edge of the tall grass, they turn into light.

11. Do the years ever run out?
    God said, I will break time's heart.
    Time ran down like an old phonograph.
    It lay flat as a carpet.
    At rest on its threads, I am learning to fly.

Nancy Willard

In The Kitchen

The fire crackles in the kitchen range, and big
disheveled clouds of steam stick their faces up
against the window-panes.

At the table, the child is writing. Leaning over him,
the father guides his wobbling hand. "Try!" he says.
"That's better—that's good." Then, "It's late."

The child writes, *Child*, and is amazed at this word
there on the page, like a friendly animal that soon,
when the ink has dried, he'll be able to stroke with
his finger.

In his best copperplate hand, the father writes *mirror*,
the curves and uprights elegantly curlicued between
the lines (he's a copying-clerk at the factory).

Mirror, the child copies; then sighs, "I'm so sleepy."
"It's snowing," the father says.

The child writes, "It's snowing," and, in his black
red-bordered pinafore, falls peacefully asleep.

Jean Joubert
Translated by Denise Levertov

The Butterfly

The last, the very last,
So richly, brightly, dazzlingly yellow.
Perhaps if the sun's tears would sing
      against a white stone....

Such, such a yellow
Is carried lightly 'way up high.
It went away I'm sure because it wished to
      kiss the world good-bye.

For seven weeks I've lived in here,
Penned up inside this ghetto.
But I have found what I love here.
The dandelions call to me
And the white chestnut branches in the court.
Only I never saw another butterfly.

That butterfly was the last one.
Butterflies don't live in here,
      in the ghetto.

Pavel Friedmann

Foul Shot

With two 60's stuck on the scoreboard
And two seconds hanging on the clock,
The solemn boy in the center of eyes,
Squeezed by silence,
Seeks out the line with his feet,
Soothes his hands along his uniform,
Gently drums the ball against the floor,
Then measures the waiting net,
Raises the ball on his right hand,
Balances it with his left,
Calms it with fingertips,
Breathes,
Crouches,
Waits,
And then through a stretching of stillness,
Nudges it upward.

The ball
Slides up and out,
Lands,
Leans,
Wobbles,
Wavers,
Hesitates,
Exasperates,
Plays it coy
Until every face begs with unsounding screams—

And then

                And then

                                And then

Right before ROAR-UP,
Dives down and through.

Edwin A. Hoey

Poop

my daughter, blake, is in kindergarten.
they are teaching her to be a docile citizen
and, incidentally, to read.
concurrently, like many of us,
she has become a trifle anal compulsive.
complications ensue.

i ask her what she has learned today.
she says, "i learned the pledge of allegiance."
"how does it go?" i ask.
"it goes," she says, "i poop allegiance
to the poop of the united poops of ameripoop."

"that's good," i say, "that's very good. what else?"
"o say can you poop, by the dawn's early poop,
what so proudly we pooped. . ."

for christmas, she improvises,
"away in a pooper, all covered with poop,
the little lord poopus
lay pooping his poop."

she has personalized other traditional favorites
as well. someone tried to teach her the "our father."
her version goes, "our pooper, who art in poopland,
hallowed be thy poop. thy poopdom poop,
thy poop be pooped, on earth as it is in poopland."

surely hemingway would feel one-upped.
surely the second pooping is at hand.

a fortune teller told us blake would be
our greatest sorrow and our greatest joy.
already it is true.

Gerald Locklin

Write a Poem

'Write a poem,' our teacher said
'A poem about an animal or a place,
Something that happened to you
In the holidays.
Better still write about yourself.
What you feel like
What's inside you
And wants to come out.'
Stephen straightaway
Began to write slowly
And went on and on
Without looking up.
John sighed and looked far away
Then suddenly snatched up his pen
And was scribbling and scribbling.
Ann tossed back her long hair
And smiled as she began.
But I sat still.
I thought of fighting cats
With chewed ears
And dogs sniffing their way along
Windy streets strewn with paper
But there seemed nothing new
To say about them...
The holidays? Nothing much happened.
And what's inside me?
Only the numbness of cold fingers.
The grey of the sky today.

John sighed again.
Peter coughed.
Papers rustled.
Pens scratched.
A blowfly was fuzzing
At a window pane.
The tittering clock
Kept snatching the minutes away
I had nothing to say.

Olive Dove

The Poem on My Pillow

I felt very small
And the house was dark
But those cookies kept calling from the kitchen
So I tiptoed downstairs
And peeked around the corner
To make sure there were no monsters.

Then I saw my dad
Alone at the kitchen table
With an open book
And a pencil and paper.
He wrote very carefully,
Then he stopped and listened . . .
And he smiled.

This morning I found this poem on my pillow.

To the Little Boy Who Hides

I listen for your breath while you sleep.
I follow your footsteps across the floor above me.
I hear the creek of wooden steps as you tiptoe down.
And I feel your fear of darkness.
Oh little son,
You need not hide from the night.
Speak out. . .
Your courage will make light.

When I read the poem I thought
My gosh . . . he heard me!
Was he angry?
Did he think I had been bad?
Then I noticed how he signed the poem . . .

To My Son . . . With Love . . . from Dad.

Brod Bagert

Desserts

Remembering Brushing My Grandmother's Hair

I see her in a ring of sewing, light
fingers on needle and hoop, elaborate
scissors shaped like a tiny stork,
the glass egg in her lap.
Her temperate mourning wore black shoes.

Released, her hair released a scent
as I imagined of ascending birds, or smoke
from a burning without source, but cool
as mist over a real country, altars in the hills.
That gray reached all the way to the floor.

A cloak, wind in a cloak, her hair
in my hands crackled and flew. I dreamed her
young and flying from some tallest room
before she had to let her power down
for something to take hold and climb.

Permanence. Rose and vine were twisted
hard in silver on the brush and mirror.
Above us, the accurate clock pinged:
always on a time there comes a sleep
stony as a tower, with the wild world beneath,

and wound like this with locked bloom tarnishing—
I brushed. She sewed or dozed. The child I was
stood shoulder-deep in dying, in a dress of falling
silver smoothed by silver, a forgetfulness
dimming the trees outside the window like a rain.

To grow to stay, to braid and bend
from one high window—
I guessed the story I would learn by heart:
how women's hands among sharp instruments
learn sleep, the frieze like metal darkening,
the land sown deep with salt.

Betty Adcock

Julian Barely Misses Zimmer's Brains

The end of winter seeped up
through our boots.
                              Julian and I
Were hunting over the fields
For the things that splayed
The deep, confident tracks in
The final snow, when Julian
Slipped on a viscid clod
And his shotgun cracked
Both barrels past my ear.

My God, my God, I see it yet!

I sit down on a cold stone
And feel my chubby brains
Float down like stuffing from
Old cushions, I feel my face
Rammed back through the grinder
Of my teeth and birds
Returning to fork me apart
Like tender meat.

Yet I am alive to tell you that
Ducks applauded overhead and game
Flicked all about, but Julian
And I had enough of shooting.

Now the only heavy footprints in
The snow are ours.
                              Spring
Has come and I am alive
With the sense that I am still alive.

Paul Zimmer

Home for Thanksgiving

The gathering family
throws shadows around us,
it is the late afternoon
of the family.

There is still enough light
to see all the way back,
but at the windows
that light is wasting away.

Soon we will be nothing
but silhouettes: the sons'
as harsh
as the fathers'.

Soon the daughters
will take off their aprons
as trees take off their leaves
for winter.

Let us eat quickly—
let us fill ourselves up.
The covers of the album are closing
behind us.

Linda Pastan

Beauty I Would Suffer For

Last week a doctor told me
anemic after an operation
to eat: ordered to indulgence,
given a papal dispensation to run
amok in Zabar's.
Yet I know that in
two weeks, a month I
will have in my nostrils
not the savor of roasting goose,
not the burnt sugar of caramel topping
the Saint-Honoré cake, not the pumpernickel
bearing up the sweet butter, the sturgeon
but again the scorched wire,
burnt rubber smell
of willpower, living
with the brakes on.

I want to pass into the boudoirs
of Rubens' women. I want to dance
graceful in my tonnage like Poussin nymphs.
Those melon bellies, those vast ripening thighs,
those featherbeds of forearms, those buttocks
placid and gross as hippopotami:
how I would bend myself
to that standard of beauty, how faithfully
I would consume waffles and sausage for breakfast
with croissants on the side, how dutifully
I would eat for supper the blackbean soup
with Madeira, followed by the fish course,
the meat course, and the Bavarian cream.
Even at intervals during the day I would
suffer an occasional éclair
for the sake of appearance.

Marge Piercy

After the Speech to the Librarians

I was speaking to the Librarians,
And now I'm standing at the end of a road,
Having taken a wrong turn going home.
I don't remember what I said.
Something about reading and writing
And not enough about listening and singing.
The gate to this dude ranch is locked,
And a dozen riderless horses are browsing
On the hillside in the gold grass.
On a post, a marsh hawk is holding still,
One eye on me and one on the field
Where hundreds of sparrow-sized water pipits
Are darting and whistling to themselves.
Not even thinking of opening a thesaurus,
I say on behalf of the Librarians, *Beautiful.*

Beyond barbed wire, a cracked water tank
And a wrecked shed: you could wait there
A long time for a school bus.
Whoever locked the gate meant No Thank You,
Not Today, but it wasn't much use.
Everything is trespassing as easily
As the hazy sunlight and these burnt-gold-breasted birds
Taking their sweet time under the hawk's eye,
Even perching beside him, extremely happy
To be where they are and what they are,
And the horses with nothing on their backs
Have opened their own gates for the winter,
And the Librarians are going back to their books
In hundreds and hundreds of schools where children
Will be reading and writing and keeping quiet
Maybe and listening to how not to be so childish.

When I wasn't looking, the hawk flew suddenly,
Skimming the field, effortlessly graceful, tilting
And scanning at low-level: he stops
Dead without slowing down, swivels
And drops into the grass, flashing white
And tawny, rises at full speed carrying nothing
And goes on soaring, slanting downhill
No higher than my head, making his sharp outcry.
The water pipits answer, thin as fence wire.
Isn't it wonderful not being dead yet?
Their breasts all hold the same air
As his and the softly whickering unsaddled horses'
And mine and the Librarians'
With which we all might sing for the children.

David Wagoner

The Poem That Wouldn't Soar

Cramped as signatures, your written
    and rewritten words keep missing
    what you mean.
                    Your paper crawls
    with black graffiti chanced
    into designs.
            Like Moslem art
    they blaze with order but cannot
    take off.
           Frowning, you put
    aside your pen as any general
    might table his surrendered sword.
Why fight this servitude?
                  Why tell
    any empty page the way you walk
    in France or how sink water slowly
    corkscrews in a whirlpool down
    a drain?
           Between the questions
    and the shrug, your pen stays mute,
    your page lies heavy with its
    epitaphs, and all your soarings
    die the death of feathers. . .
                  Later,
    your son selects your failure
    of a poem as his own and folds it
    into wings.
            You watch him
    walk it to the wind and aim it
    like an archer at the sun.
                  Flung.
    the paper that was merely paper
    inked with your defeats becomes
    the poem it was meant to be,
    and, like a horse with wings as free
    and wild as the air, takes off.

Samuel Hazo

The Poem as Striptease

There was a difference of opinion
afterwards
as to just how far
she went.

Philip Dacey

The Junior Highschool Band Concert

When our semi-conductor
Raised his baton, we sat there
Gaping at *Marche Militaire*,
Our mouth-opening number.
It seemed faintly familiar
(We'd rehearsed it all that winter),
But we attacked in such a blur,
No army anywhere
On its stomach or all fours
Could have squeezed through our crossfire.

I played cornet, seventh chair
Out of seven, my embouchure
A glorified Bronx cheer
Through that three-keyed keyhole stopper
And neighborhood window-slammer
Where mildew fought for air
At every exhausted corner,
My fingering still unsure
After scaling it for a year
Except on the spit-valve lever.

Each straight-faced mother and father
Retested his moral fibre
Against our traps and slurs
And the inadvertent whickers
Paradiddled by our snares,
And when the brass bulled forth
A blare fit to horn over
Jericho two bars sooner
Than Joshua's harsh measures,
They still had the nerve to stare.

By the last lost chord, our director
Looked older and soberer.
No doubt, in his mind's ear
Some band somewhere
In some Music of some Sphere
Was striking a note as pure
As the wishes of Franz Schubert,
But meanwhile here we were:
A lesson in everything minor,
Decomposing our first composer.

David Wagoner

The Hug

A woman is reading a poem on the street
and another woman stops to listen. We stop too,
with our arms around each other. The poem
is being read and listened to out here
in the open. Behind us
no one is entering or leaving the houses.

Suddenly a hug comes over me and I'm
giving it to you, like a variable star shooting light
off to make itself comfortable, then
subsiding. I finish but keep on holding
you. A man walks up to us and we know he hasn't
come out of nowhere, but if he could, he
would have. He looks homeless because of how
he needs. "Can I have one of those?" he asks you,
and I feel you nod. I'm surprised,
surprised you don't tell him how
it is—that I'm yours, only
yours, etc., exclusive as a nose to
its face. Love—that's what we're talking about, love
that nabs you with "for me
only" and holds on.

So I walk over to him and put my
arms around him and try to
hug him like I mean it. He's got an overcoat on
so thick I can't feel
him past it. I'm starting the hug
and thinking, "How big a hug is this supposed to be?
How long shall I hold this hug?" Already
we could be eternal, his arms falling over my
shoulders, my hands not
meeting behind his back, he is so big!

I put my head into his chest and snuggle
in. I lean into him. I lean my blood and my wishes
into him. He stands for it. This is his
and he's starting to give it back so well I know he's
getting it. This hug. So truly, so tenderly
we stop having arms and I don't know if
my lover has walked away or what, or
if the woman is still reading the poem, or the houses—
what about them?—the houses.

Clearly, a little permission is a dangerous thing.
But when you hug someone you want it
to be a masterpiece of connection, the way the button
on his coat will leave the imprint of
a planet in my cheek
when I walk away. When I try to find some place
to go back to.

Tess Gallagher

Fruits & Cheeses

Apple

I open the orange photo album
And they're there, family in black and whites,
Off-color color prints. I like the one of
My brother, sister, and me standing by a car
Fender. We're like bushes set not quite straight
In the ground, thin and crooked, and we are shading
Our eyes in childish salutes. The shadow
Of our mother behind the camera
Is lean. The ground at our feet is sandy.
The houses behind us are white, rickety white
From thirty years of rain. I like this
Photograph, circa 1956. We were new
In our bodies and the people we loved were still alive.
My uncle had a Model-T that I tried to help
Get started. Instead of pushing, I pulled
From the front fender and was dragged up the alley,
The engine whirring warm air into my face. My uncle
Stopped, pulled me up, swatted a cloud
Of dust from my pants. My brother
Was tricking me then, too.
He would say, Captain Kangaroo
Lives in that house,
And of course I would climb the brick steps and knock.
He would point, That kid said you were black,
And I would pick up the nearest rock.
I didn't catch on right away
That meanness was part of the family.
I kept going where people told me to go.
One day my mother sent me to Charlie's Market
For an apple pie, the kind in which one end peeks
From a sleeve of waxed paper. I gave Charlie
The fifteen cents. I started
Home staring at the end of the apple pie,
Little snout of sugary crust.
I wanted very badly to take one bite.
I walked slowly thinking, Just one bite.

Mother would say, You had yours without asking
But you should wait next time.
She wouldn't be too mad. I worried
About the apple pie, walked slowly
Around the block the long way,
And when I couldn't stand it anymore,
I took a bite. A sugary flake fell from my mouth.
It was sweet. I took a second bite
And three lines worried my brow.
I took the pie out of the paper
Wrapper, and turned it the other way
So the eaten side didn't show.
But I kept walking around the block, a kid
Lost in a neighborly orbit, and staring
At the pie. Again I couldn't stand it.
My mouth opened when my hand
Forced the pie to my face.
Now both sides were ruined,
Chunks gone out. How could I say,
Mom, I don't know how it got that way.
I hid in a vacant lot
Behind a stack of greenish boards,
Companion to the scurry of red ants at my feet.
I don't remember ever getting up to go back home.

Laughter is another sin. How funny
To think I could eat from both ends
And get away with it. God is at least that voice
Inside us that says *yes* and *no*.
God said *no*, and I hid behind a stack
Of boards. God said *yes* when
I tried to help Uncle with his old black car
And didn't let me die under a dusty wheel.
It's been that way ever since. Yes.
And no, never a maybe. Because of this,

I once tried to steal from Charlie's Market.
I stood at a tier of thirteen kinds of candy,
And I closed my hand around a Baby Ruth,
Then opened it very quickly
Because it was wrong. I was a boy,
No brighter than the penny
In my pocket. I closed my hand around
The candy again, then opened it.
God would know, my mother would know,
And certainly Charlie who was leaning his elbows
On the glass counter. I didn't see him watching.
My small eyes stared at the candy,
First temptation of the greedy tooth.
My hand opened and closed around the Baby Ruth
Several more times. I kept thinking
All I have to do is pick it up
And it'll be mine.

Gary Soto

The Apple

I've tossed an apple at you; if you can love me,
take it. Give me your girlhood in exchange.
If you think what I hope you won't, though,
take it, look at it:
consider how briefly its beauty is going to last.

Plato

Oranges

The first time I walked
With a girl, I was twelve,
Cold, and weighted down
With two oranges in my jacket.
December. Frost cracking
Beneath my steps, my breath
Before me, then gone,
As I walked toward
Her house, the one whose
Porch light burned yellow
Night and day, in any weather.
A dog barked at me, until
She came out pulling
At her gloves, face bright
With rouge. I smiled,
Touched her shoulder, and led
Her down the street, across
A used car lot and a line
Of newly planted trees,
Until we were breathing
Before a drugstore. We
Entered, the tiny bell
Bringing a saleslady
Down a narrow aisle of goods.
I turned to the candies
Tiered like bleachers,
And asked what she wanted—
Light in her eyes, a smile
Starting at the corners
Of her mouth. I fingered
A nickel in my pocket,
And when she lifted a chocolate
That cost a dime,
I didn't say anything.
I took the nickel from
My pocket, then an orange,

And set them quietly on
The counter. When I looked up,
The lady's eyes met mine,
And held them, knowing
Very well what it was all
About.

      Outside,
A few cars hissing past,
Fog hanging like old
Coats between the trees.
I took my girl's hand
In mine for two blocks,
Then released it to let
Her unwrap the chocolate.
I peeled my orange
That was so bright against
The gray of December
That, from some distance,
Someone might have thought
I was making a fire in my hands.

Gary Soto

August Pickings

"I hear the swamp berries are ready,"
Dad announced with a grin.

I knew that meant
riding to Spotswood
just Dad and me
picking in the hot August afternoon
until sun and pails grew heavy
popping more berries into my mouth
than into my pail.

I knew that meant
keeping out by the road
—there Dad said it was safe—
worrying he'd get lost
deep where berries grow bigger
knowing all the while, though, he'd
pour some of his in my pail
trying "to make things even"
cause he didn't allow me in too far.

I knew that meant
eating fat berry fritters
with fresh lemony sauce
thinking even then
how it was like him
gentling up supper with
no bucks killed, no dove either,
smiling, proud as any hunter,
when Mom praised the size our catch.

Strange. God also went picking
one August. Plucked Dad from us
like a ripe berry when he was
sweetest, most dear.

I no longer go berrying. Instead,
remembering, I pick pails of words
spilling them over into poems
trying "to make things even"
cause he didn't allow me in too far.

Joyce Armstrong Carroll

After Lunch

the mind sags
like a filled hammock
strung between two great Oaks
heavy from the morning
weighted with fruit and grain
the stone must be soaked
in fresh cool words
until it dissolves in watery delight
shimmering in minute golden specks
as it rises from lethargy
ablaze with the alchemy
of poetic transformation
ready to intermingle
and regather
in new patterns

Carol M. Siskovic

The Purpose of Poetry

This old man grazed thirty head of cattle
in a valley just north of the covered bridge
on the Mississinewa, where the reservoir
stands today. Had a black border collie
and a half-breed sheep dog with one eye.
The dogs took the cows to pasture each morning
and brought them home again at night
and herded them into the barn. The old man
would slip a wooden bar across both doors.
One dog slept on the front porch, one on the back.

He was waiting there one evening
listening to the animals coming home
when a man from the courthouse stopped
to tell him how the new reservoir
was going to flood all his property.
They both knew he was too far up in years
to farm anywhere else. He had a daughter
who lived in Florida, in a trailer park.
He should sell now and go stay with her.
The man helped bar the doors before he left.

He had only known dirt under his fingernails
and trips to town on Saturday mornings
since he was a boy. Always he had been around
cattle, and trees, and land near the river.
Evenings by the barn he could hear the dogs
talking to each other as they brought in
the herd; and the cows answering them.
It was the clearest thing he knew. That night
he shot both dogs and then himself.
The purpose of poetry is to tell us about life.

Jared Carter

Acknowledgments

Philip Dacey, for "The Poem as Striptease" Reprinted by permission of the author, first appeared in *Bits*.

Olga Samples Davis, for "Sister Girl" from A *Time to be Born* by Olga Samples Davis published by Pecan Grove Press Copyright © 1991.

Angela de Hoyos, for "Virgin Mother" by Angela de Hoyos is reprinted with permission from the publisher of *Woman, Woman* (Houston: Arte Publico Press - University of Houston, 1985).

Olive Dove, for "Write a Poem" from *Drumming on the Sky*, a BBC anthology. Reprinted by permission of the author.

John Eubanks, for "i need a new prompt" from *Second Stories*, by John Eubanks, 1994. Reprinted with permission of the author.

Robert A. Fink, for "An Old Man's Passing" from *Azimuth Points*, 1981 Texas Review Poetry Award Chapbook, reprinted with permission.

Pavel Friedmann, for "The Butterfly" from I *Never Saw Another Butterfly* by U. S. Holocaust Memorial Councile, edited by Hana Volavkova. Copyright © 1978, 1993 by Artia, Prague. Compilation Copyright © 1993 by Schocken Books Inc. Reprinted by permission of Schocken Books, distributed by Pantheon Books, a division of Random House, Inc.

Robert Frost, for "The Road Not Taken" from *The Poetry of Robert Frost* edited by Edward Connery Lathem. "Out, Out--" from *The Poetry of Robert Frost* edited by Edward Connery Lathem. Copyright © 1936 by Robert Frost. Copyright © 1964 by Lesley Frost Ballantine. Copyright © 1969 by Henry Holt and Co., Inc.

Tess Gallagher, for "The Hug" Copyright © 1987 by Tess Gallagher. Reprinted from *Amplitude* with the permission of Graywolf Press, Saint Paul, Minnesota.

Robert Hayden, for "The Whipping." Reprinted from *Collected Poems of Robert Hayden*, edited by Frederick Glaysher, with the permission of Liveright Publishing Corporation. Copyright © 1966 by Robert Hayden.

Samuel Hazo, for "The Poem That Wouldn't Soar" from *To Paris*, New Directions, 1981. Reprinted by permission of the author.

Edwin A. Hoey, for "Foul Shot." Special permission granted by READ®, published by Weekly Reader Corporation. Copyright © renewed 1989, 1962 by Weekly Reader Corporation. All rights reserved.

Andrew Hudgins, for "At the Piano" from *Saints and Strangers*. Copyright © 1985 by Andrew Hudgins. Reprinted by permission of Houghton Mifflin Co. All rights

University of Chicago Press, reprinted by permission of publisher.

Naomi Shihab Nye, for "Valentine for Ernest Mann" and "What is Supposed to Happen" Copyright © 1994, by Naomi Shihab Nye. Reprinted from *Red Suitcase*, by Naomi Shihab Nye, with the permission of BOA Editions, Ltd. 92 Park Ave., Brockport, NY 14420

Sharon Olds, for "Last Words" from *The Father* by Sharon Olds Copyright © 1992 by Sharon Olds. Reprinted by permission of Alfred A. Knopf, Inc.

Linda Pastan, for "The Myth of Perfectability" and "The Bookstall." Reprinted from *Heroes in Disguise* by Linda Pastan, with the permission of W.W. Norton & Company, Inc. Copyright © 1991 by Linda Pastan, for "Home for Thanksgiving" Copyright by Linda Pastan. This poem first appeared in *Setting The Table*. Dryad Press, for "To a Daughter Leaving Home." Reprinted from *The Imperfect Paradise* by Linda Pastan, with the permission of W. W. Norton & Company, Inc. Copyright © 1988 by Linda Pastan.

Marge Piercy, for "The Poet Dreams of a Nice Warm Motel" by Marge Piercy. Copyright © 1978 by Marge Piercy and Middlemarsh, Inc. Reprinted by permission of the Wallace Literary Agency, Inc, "Beauty I Would Suffer For" by Marge Piercy. Copyright © 1976,1978 by Marge Piercy and Middlemarsh, Inc. Originally appeared in *Massachusetts Review*, #1, 1976. Reprinted by permission of the Wallace Literary Agency, Inc.

Plato, for "The Apple." The compilers acknowledge that receiving permission from Plato will not happen, but wish to acknowledge him and his work which is in the realm of public domain.

Freda Quenneville, for "Mother's Biscuits" Copyright © Freda Quenneville. Reprinted by permission of the author.

George Roberts, for "while dissecting frogs in biology class scrut discovers the intricacies of the scooped neckline in his lab partner's dress." Reprinted from *Scut* by George Roberts (Holy Cow! Press, 1983) by permission of the publisher.

Mona Robinson, for "Repercussion." Reprinted with permission of the author.

Duncan Campbell Scott, for "The Forsaken." The work of Duncan Campbell Scott is printed with the permission of John G. Aylan, Ottawa, Canada.

Shel Silverstein, for "Little Abigail and the Beautiful Pony" from *A Light in the Attic* by Shel Silverstein. Copyright © 1981 by Evil Eye Music, Inc., permission granted by HarperCollins Publishers.

Carol Siskovic, for "After Lunch" with permission of the author.

Gary Soto, for "Apple" for "Oranges" from *New and Selected Poems* by Gary Soto

Corporation. Copyright © 1974 by Nancy Willard. "How to Stuff a Pepper" originally published in Kayak., for "In Praise of ABC." Reprinted from *Carpenter of the Sun* by Nancy Willard with the permission of Liveright Publishing Corporation. Copyright © 1974 by Nancy Willard. "In Praise of ABC" originally published in *Hudson River Anthology*. "For You, Who Didn't Know" reprinted from *Carpenter of the Sun* by Nancy Willard, with the permission of Liveright Publishing Corporation. Originally published in *Shenandoah*. Copyright © 1974 by Nancy Willard.

Edward E. Wilson, for "Revival Week" and "The Unchosen" by permission of the author.

Paul Zimmer, for "Julian Barely Misses Zimmer's Brains." Reprinted by permission of the University of Arkansas Press from *The Big Blue Train* by Paul Zimmer.

The Cover:

The rendering of a photograph on the cover was done by Edward E. Wilson. The original photograph is by Mark Ferri. Mr. Ferri graciously and generously granted permission for the use of his photograph to be rendered in such a way. The compilers are grateful for his allowance of such use. While the compilers appreciated his fine photograph, they wished a more impressionistic image rather than a photographic one. The process was completed by Adobe Photoshop™ 3.0.5.

Index of Poems

Index of Poets